THINK YOU CAN TEACH?

THINK YOU CAN TEACH?

A survival guide for new middle
school teachers

Leon Avrech

ILLUSTRATIONS BY GREGORY MOSHER

Library of Congress Control Number:		2007900718
ISBN:	Hardcover	978-1-4257-6754-9
	Softcover	978-1-4257-6749-5

This book was printed in the United States of America.

To order additional copies of this book, contact:
Xlibris Corporation
1-888-795-4274
www.Xlibris.com
Orders@Xlibris.com
38853

CONTENTS

RECIPE FOR SUCCESS
INGREDIENTS

APPENDIX

DEDICATION

To my wife, Beverly, who supported my career in education. She chaperoned thirty seven years of school dances and graduations.

To my daughters, Sherie and Karen, who allowed me the time to grade papers and folders when they were growing up.

To Sherie's children, Cassandra and Ryan.

To Karen's children, Kevin, Jeffrey, and Samantha

ACKNOWLEDGEMENTS

My wife who always supported me teaching and was always proud of my profession. She was never jealous of friends and acquaintances who in one way or another displayed their money and their higher income. She knew that I had the best job and was doing what I loved. For almost 40 years she listened to the daily classroom stories I told.

Kids and grandkids who always thought I had a wonderful career. My daughters never envied those with more income to spend. They never once said "how come we don't have more money?"

Of course maybe it was because I had second jobs. Teachers good and bad, crying and happy. Teachers going off campus and never returning. "Where did that person go?", we all wondered. Teachers that stayed home on Back to School days,parent conference days/nights and Open House. No one can be sick on those days year after year. That is no coincidence. Obviously, you don't want to be like them.

Filthy rooms, strewn litter, graffitti walls, bare walls, food on the floor. I knew I had to tell new teachers that they must not let that happen. That is not conducive to learning. It makes a bad impression on fellow teachers, parents, and visitors.

Sink or swim when hired. Those that swam and those that sunk can teach us alot. Those that were successful and those that were not had certain characteristics. I will show you how to swim and love your career. I, also, acknowlege the hundreds of wonderful and dedicated teachers that I have met over the years. They are amazing people.

PROLOGUE

As I closed the classroom door for the last time, tears came to my eyes. I thought of all the wonderful years in middle school as administrator and teacher. Thirty seven years in middle school to be exact. "How did you survive that long?" people would ask. "That age group is impossible to teach, and all those raging hormones too. They test you to the limit." Of course those people don't know that is why that age level is so much fun to teach.

I said goodbye to the now empty desks, the four walls, and the closet which for years held my precious stuff that I would use for lessons every year. I said goodbye to the students who were hanging around. "Good luck Mr. Avrech, we will miss you. My brother and sister in the fourth and fifth grades will not get you as a teacher. I wonder who will teach them." I wondered that too. Some new staff member or someone who wants to teach "my subject" for a change from what they have been teaching.

I locked the classroom door and checked the door, something that I've been doing as habit for years. "Never leave the classroom door open," the principal would remind the staff. I slowly walked across the patio to the parking lot on that warm June day for the last time. I walked across confetti, balloons, and candy wrappers as the kids left campus after celebrating the end of the year. Funny, I didn't feel like celebrating. As the sun beat down on the warm pavement, teachers packing supplies for the next year yelled out, "have a nice retirement." "Lucky you."

Much of my classroom supplies I left in the room except for personal supplies that I took home in boxes. "I better keep this organized", I thought, but couldn't think of a reason. "Would they call me back?" I wondered. After all who had all this experience, principal and teacher for so many years. Surely they would call on my experience. I was wrong. There were others who would become teachers and learn on their feet as I did. Not all was left in that classroom, on that campus in that closet. There were memories mostly good, some bad, not terrible just bad. I turned the AC on and let the car interior cool. The outside temperature was 86 degrees. I thought that the interior of the car with the sun blazing through the windows felt like my classroom all those years without air conditioning. Air conditioning was too expensive on the tight District budget. Maybe in the future. Well the air conditioning arrived the year I retired. So, I got some comfort at least. There were other challenges in the classroom besides teaching the kids. Arriving at school at 7: A.M. on a chilly morning and finding out the heat did not work again. The custodian came by and said that the old heater needs a part that if they still make it, it will not arrive for several days. Then District maintenance will come out and fix it. The crickets on the floor were not inviting as you had your lessons ready to put on the board. It's ok I thought, I'll kick some out the door with my shoe and the few others some student will pick up. Some boys love to pick them up showing their bravado and tossing them out the door.

The memory of the morning crickets is something that I would like to forget.

The memories of the vice principals sometimes called assistant principal ran through my head as a police cruiser came by. Maybe the principal called because of rowdy last day behavior or maybe he came by for chit chat and a morning coffee.

Some vice principals were very strict and others were not. For most it was a necessary stop on the way up to being principal or a district office administrator like Curriculum Director, Human Resources Director (I prefer Personnel Director), or Superintendent. Vice Principal was not a position teachers wanted to be for any length of time. "I can be principal soon", they thought.

When there is an opening for principal in the District, they quickly applied. They became very angry when they were passed over for someone else, especially if that someone came from out of the District. I recalled many vice principals, some helped a great deal with excellent consequences for the students which helped modify behavior. There were also those who called a teacher on the phone and said, "Control your kids. Don't keep sending them to the office. I'm busy." Most of the teachers at lunch and break would criticize the VP for lack of a good discipline strategy. The student I sent was sent back. That's it. The kid was even smirking. Some support you and some don't.

Many VP's will at least keep the student for the remainder of the period. "Call the parents," you are told. Tomorrow the same student comes walking into your classroom. A new adventure for you.

Principals are not all the same. Some Principals are friendly and eager to help the teachers, others are more of the leave the staff alone type of personality. Many principals must have the once a week staff meeting whether one is really needed or not. Others will have a staff meeting when there is something meaningful to present. My experience as a teacher is that I had supportive and friendly principals. Of course it helps if you are able to control your class and have positive results on mandated state tests. A principal may have a planned formal observation of your teaching which is a visit in which notes are written and the information is part of your end of year evaluation. If you are fortunate, you will be given the date and time of the visit so you can make sure you are prepared. "The principal is coming to visit," you tell your students. You hope the students will be on their best behavior. Visits may last the entire period. As the air conditioning cooled my car, I thought about the dedicated principals that I had during my teaching career. I was fortunate.

The police cruiser left with no student in handcuffs, thank goodness. It was a just a visit and a cup of coffee or a cold drink from the facutly room vending machine.

The kids that I saw in my teaching career in middle school where 95% good. This shocks people when I tell them because the bad behavior kids take so much time, energy, and get the publicity in the neighborhood. "Did you hear about the fight at school today" spreads like a prairie fire in the neighborhood. Most of kids' behavior is not bad. I thought of those that spoke out of turn in class. Those that did not do homework or even show up. "The invisible student is not here again today". On the day of the week the student is in class, "I'm here today so what did I miss for the last five days?" I thought of the kids that greeted me first thing in the morning standing by the classroom door. "Can I come in and help you?" they ask. I thought of the students, not many, who are unable to reach. "Where is your pencil, paper, & book?" I ask. They do not attempt to do the assignment.

"The assignment is due at the end of class. Get going." They don't care if the assignment is due in five minutes or five days. I feel bad for those kids knowing that they have hurt their future. They don't care if they receive an "F" in the class. Sad! It is important to continue to help these students as much as you can. "Stop playing with your Little Kitty toys and do the assignment." The kids are at all maturity levels. There are wonderful memories of students with straight A's. Their classwork, homework, projects, tests, etc. all A's. "My parents expect perfect grades and that's what I get." I loved to show that student's work to other teachers, visitors, and administrators. "What a pleasure, what fun to teach", I thought. I must show the work of these wonderful students. They make every day special. They are very proud of the superior work that they do. I am so proud of them. "This is like college work," I tell my family and friends. So it's goodbye to the kids, my students, all different yet so much alike. Every year the honor students, the students that don't care, the students that are so well behaved and those that are not. The perfect work on assignments and tests and those that turn in sloppy work. The ones that strive to learn every day and those that try not to learn. Some are never sent to "the office" and some sit in the vice principal's office every day. They are to be loved and cared for. All of them.

You are to be commended for selecting the middle school/junior high for your teaching career. The students need you. You will have an exciting, never a dull moment, never a dull year as I showed you in the prologue. There is much more.

I've heard their music and danced their dances from the Beatles to Disco to the Macarena to Break Dancing and Hip Hop and loved it all.

What I can do to help our profession is to help YOU become a successful teacher and to walk proud and confident.

You are a tremendous influence on the youngsters in your class, their success is your success. Years from now, when your students are well into their adult years and they call your name saying, "I remember your great class. I will never forget it." You smile broadly and get a warm comfortable feeling of achievement inside.

Walking in the mall and hearing your name, you turn around, "Who can that be calling me?" You turn around and it's one of your students with the parents. "Hi, I love your class. It's my favorite." "Thank you very much. I appreciate you saying that." You smile broadly to the parents and your day has been made. When you retire the same thing happens but the parents are your former students and are walking with their children or young ones in a stroller. Now THAT is an experience. You feel old, but you know that you have made a difference. They have their own family and career.

Two of many recent experiences I would like to share with you. I was sitting at McDonalds one morning and a woman across the aisle at a larger table was telling her 5th grade son and 3rd grade daughter that they were going shopping after they finished their choclate milk. She looked at me and said, "Aren't you Mr. Avrech? You were my 8th grade teacher." Wow, she remembered so far back.

Not only is she a mom and wife, but has a big job in a computer company in Silicon Valley. I can't recall her job title, but it was one which she is making considerably more than I did as a teacher. It was wonderful to be remembered. Many people who work in the high tech industry will not be remembered in that way. Another successful person.

In a large "big box" store a man in his thirties was pushing a shopping cart with his two children. "I remember you", he said. "I had you in middle school." Sometimes you wonder if you have to duck or run, but that never happens. "You really helped me," he said. "I never forgot your class."

"Do you remember my friends in that class,"he asks as he mentions several names. I told him I remembered them, but I really wasn't sure. Many students over those many years. I know they all want to be remembered. Some apologize for their behavior. "I'm sorry," they say.

MY EDUCATION AND EXPERIENCE

**Bachelor of Arts University of Calif., Berkeley
**Master of Arts-Educ. San Jose State University.
**teaching middle school
**department chairman
**teachers association president
**summer school principal, opening a new school
**assistant principal grades 6th-8th
**principal grades 6th-8th
**mentor teacher District and County

I have prepared this guide with 37 years experience. Take advantage of my experience and avoid the pitfalls while gaining confidence.

Some of you knew you wanted to be a teacher since you were playing school as a child. Many like me were unsure of what career path to follow. It was my sophmore year at Berkeley that I found my calling. I was walking through Dwinelle Hall, the building where the professors had their offices. As I walked and looked inside the office doors that were open, I saw professors helping students with their assignments. My interest was peaked as I continued walking to the office where I needed help. I was thinking, "Now that's what I'd like to do. Teach and help people learn." That was a good idea. I knew that family and friends would immediately say that there is no money in that job.

"What about a lawyer, dentist, doctor, or business tycoon," they would say. "All that college and no big money after graduating." I wasn't swayed.

BE AWARE OR BEWARE OF THESE:

*Orientation
*Your first day
*What they didn't teach you in college
*Organizing your classroom
*Classroom management
*Curriculum
*Writing lesson plans
*Setting objectives
*How not to use the assistant principal & principal
*Classroom observation
*End of year evaluation
*Yard duty strategies
*Parent communication
    **Back to School Night
    **letters home
    **Open House
    **conferences
    **phone calls
*Creating a positive but relaxed atmosphere
*Setting goals for students
*Gaining Tenure
*Discipline
*Being organized and consistent
*Homework

*Grades & citizenship
*Extra-curricular activities
*You and the Teachers Union
*Activities
Standardized tests
*Music in the classroom
*Letter to your students.
*Preparing your substitute

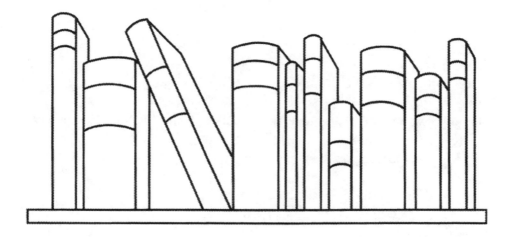

FIRST THINGS FIRST

CURRICULUM

What are you teaching?

What is your schedule?

What is your grade level?

Ability grouped?

Do you have a textbook? Is there one for each of the students in your class? Teachers edition?

What other resources are available to you, such as supplimentary materials, videos, software, etc.?

Have you studied the District curriculum guide?

Have you reviewed what it is you are teaching?

Have you consulted with teachers in your department as to what is expected?

Have you seeked their assistance as to long range plans?

Do you have appropriate supplies to meet your plans?

What are rules for use of the computers?

Can you answer the above questions in the affirmative? Are you sure?

During Orientation, your first days at school, be sure you cover the above topics if you have not done so before your first required day.

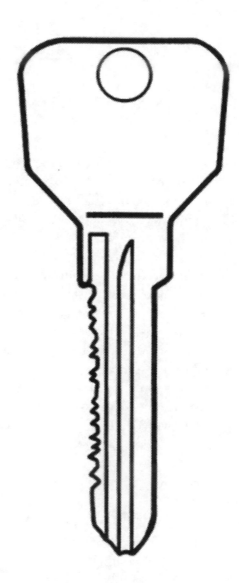

ORIENTATION

You have been looking with anticipation for this day ever since you decided that you wanted to teach. You have had the interviews and been hired and now it is here, the day you report to your school. You look in the mirror. Are your clothes appropriate? How does your hair look? Will the faculty like you? And then the fear strikes, what if I don't fit in? When you arrive, the school secretary tells you the time and place of the Orientation Meeting, usually in the library or in a classroom. If in the classroom, squeezing your adult body in to middle school desks can be a task in itself. Remember you don't want to make a scene. The secretary directs you to the faculty lounge and tells you to have coffee. You may not drink coffee and you certainly did not think to bring your own coffe cup. So you sit, you watch, as the veteran teachers arrive and tell others about their summer vacation. You did not have one. You were going on interviews and taking classes. You will be mostly ignored by the veterans. Other new teachers if any will introduce themselves to you as you wonder when the staff will talk to you. You get a lump in your throat when you overhear other teachers say, "another person thinks they can teach here."

Maybe he/she can coach. We always have problems finding volleyball, track, and basketball coaches.

Maybe the new staff will supervise the dances or yearbook or student council. Eventually, you hear the announcement for all teachers to report to the faculty meeting in the library. Yes, they called you a teacher, how wonderful you feel. You find your place in the library looking for the friendliest faces and those probably of your gender.

The principal welcomes everyone and introduces you, the new staff member. Everyone gives you a cordial applause thinking "good luck to you" because it's sink or swim. You smile and look down at the stack of handouts being delivered to everyone. Immediately, you notice the veterans looking at the calendar for the year already counting the days to the first vacation. "Do we get off Columbus Day?" They are also looking at the class lists counting the number of students and girls and boys. A sigh of relief for those who have some classes with more girls because it is generally agreed that those classes will have less discipline problems. "Have a great year," says the principal after the more than two hour staff meeting highlighted by the yearly debate on what to do about tardies. When are students sent to the office and what is the punishment for tardy students? The vets say the principal could have recorded the meeting because it's the same as the last five years. To you it's new and you are excited as you get your room key. You ask for directions and you begin the journey to your room. Is it air conditioned, does the heater work, will I hear the teacher next door, are there supplies in the room, is there a closet for my stuff, are there windows, do I share the room with another teacher?

You take out your key and enter the classroom.

Your classroom. You look at the 35 desks and anticipate all the great learning that will take place and how much the students will learn from you. You look around your classroom and see the bare walls and envision the "bulletin board" you need to put up.

You look in the closet for supplies but there are none. You ask the teacher next door about supplies and are told you need to order them from the District Supply Catalog sticking to the budget allowed for your room. You are told that supples will be delivered in about 10 working days. You will need to plan a visit to the local office supply store for crayons, scissors, pencils, thumb tacks,etc. You will not get paid until the first of the month, but you must purchase the necessary items before the students arrive. Your shrinking checkbook will shrink some more. You brought your box of desk items to personalize your room.

You will look for the number of textbooks you will need and go get them. Hopefully, you beat the veterans so you can get the number you need so that students do not have to share. Now is the time to re read "FIRST THINGS FIRST", and make sure each item is covered.

Put the lesson plan book on your desk and begin to write the lessons for the week. "I wonder how much work they can do in one hour?"you ask yourself. Write the classroom rules that you expect the students to follow. Put them on the bulletin board. Now you have the first "decoration" on your bare walls. WRITE THE FIRST DAY LESSONS ON THE CHALKBOARD, YOUR NAME AND SUBJECT. Take a deep breath and get ready for your first day of instruction.

THE FIRST DAY

Make sure your classroom looks inviting. Bulletin Board should be up and related to what you are teaching. If you are sharing a classroom, ask the other teacher for space. Greet students like you are excited to see them!! Welcome the students to your class and tell them what they are going to learn. Their "Locater Card" should indicate your class and period number. Seat your students alphabetically. This way you can learn names more quickly and maintain better discipline. Adjustments will be made later for a myriad of reasons. Take roll very carefully.

Forms for reduced price and free lunch should be on a counter or table for easy pickup. Don't announce,"Who gets free lunch?"

Seating idea for first week: 5x8 card on desk/table with student name. Eliminates reading and mispronouncing names. Have the student read the name on the card and ask if they have a "nickname". Don't assume gender from a name: Sunny, Jolly, Chevrolet, Sotha, Adonnis, Sara, Tuyet, Thu, Bao, Sam, and Dana are examples.

DO NOT DISTRIBUTE BOOKS THE FIRST DAY.

DO NOT ENTER STUDENTS IN THE GRADE BOOK.

Your class may change because of students' changing schedules and for students and parents who "didn't know school started already."

The bell rings for the students to report to class. You are standing in front of the classroom keeping your eyes on the students at all times. You are thinking which one of these kids will be my best student and which one will cause me sleepless nights. "Students, you see a card on your desk with your name on it in alphabetical order so I can learn your name much faster. Please remember where you are seated for the next few days. We will go down the rows (or each table) for you to say your name. Cards with no one at the desk will be marked absent. Thank you."

"Notice I have posted the classroom rules. In every class you will be hearing about rules because they might be different for each teacher.

If you look on the board, you will see what we are going to do today. In a week, I'll assign you a textbook, but for now do not take them out of the room."

Make sure you have enough work for the students even though it is the first day. If you don't, students will get restless and your discipline problems begin. In general, students are fairly well behaved and quiet the first few days.

Free and reduced price lunch applications should be on a table for those who need one. They know who they are because they had them last year.

When the dismissal bell rings, do not let them stand up and leave. It is up to you to set the tone. You dismiss them, otherwise the day will surely come when the bell will ring before the lesson is done or papers collected.

"CLASS DISMISSED. SAME PLACES TOMORROW."

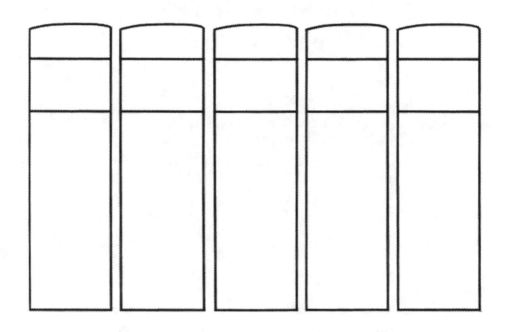

PREPARING YOUR LESSONS
LESSON PLANS

Make sure you write lesson plans!

Your lesson planning book should be on your desk!

Lesson plans should always be available for a sub.

The lesson plans are not in your head, they are in your plan book. They can also be on the computer.

Plan your year, what you think you will cover and using the district calendar outline your year. Of course this will be updated and changed throughout the year. Consult District/State Framework as close as possible. Consult with other teachers as to the length of time for each unit.

Check dates for standardized tests.

Write lessons for each week. Be specific on what you want to teach and your objectives for the lesson. The best time to write weekly plans is Friday after school or Sunday night. Your principal may collect them. Write neatly in case a sub. has to read them. In case you become ill at night, you can email your substitute updated lessons.

DO NOT COME TO CLASS UNPREPARED!!

Update plans with suggestions to yourself for next year. Did the assignment accomplish what you thought it would?

Do not show R or X rated videos. PG is risky!!

Pre screen all movies, show none from students.

Do not play music with sex or violence lyrics.

Make your students feel that your subject is important. You might even wear a tee shirt with something about your subject. You may find current news or magazine articles related to your subject. Some videos may add enrichment to your class and help with understanding the lesson.

CLASSROOM MANAGEMENT
THE DO'S, THE DON'TS, THE WHAT IFS

Be organized! Be ready to begin at the bell!

Beginning your lesson at the bell or shortly before will encourage promptness to class.

Dismiss students on time so they are not tardy to the next class.

Have a clear discipline plan.

Post your classroom rules and read them the first day.

Never be late to class or leave the door open.

Lock the classroom when you leave the room.

Greet students at the door or acknowledge them when they enter the room.

Be consistent in discipline. Never hit a student.

Do not "lose it" in front of the class. Walk over and quietly talk to the disruptive student.

You DO want your students to enjoy your class.

Sending a stream of students to the office is not a good idea because it shows problems are beyond you. If you want to get rehired, sending students to the office for non severe problems is not the way.

Allowing the office to handle discipline for your class shows your students that you can not control them. It also makes the principal aware of classroom control problems. Be firm from day one.

An incident happened in your classroom?? Call the parent at home or work before the student gets home. Notify the assistant principal or principal!

Be honest and sincere. Do not lie.

Assign homework! Parents want to see that your class has homework. Weekends free is fine.

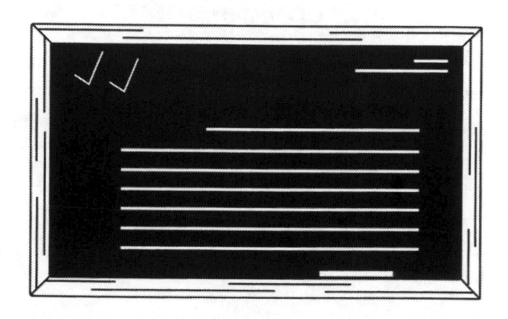

MORE DO'S AND DON'TS

Praise your students early and often. They will work up to your expectations.

You are teaching subjects and children.

Continue to work on a positive atmosphere.

Never embarass or degrade a student in front of the class.

Do not do in your classroom what you insist the students must not do. Example: chew gum, eat candy or cake, drink coffee, eat a sandwich, etc.

Water bottles for drinking appears ok unless misused. Some drinks are clear like water. You think it doesn't happen? It does!

Be sensitive to students if tired from standardized tests or excessive heat. Cool it!

Do not talk toooo much. Students will tune you out. They get bored very fast.

Tell students that they can succeed in your class and that you are there to help them not flunk them.

Don't talk over dismissal bell.

Use a variety of classroom activities: (multiple intelligences) reading, writing, oral, drawing, hands on, etc. etc.

BE OVER PLANNED. Be planned for more than the class period. You can never have to much to do. It always can be extended into the next day's plans.

SUCCESS BREEDS SUCCESS!!

Show trust. You may have one of your lower achieving students pass out paper, or pass back assignments, tests, etc.

Before a major test, tell the students what is going to be tested. Review. Help them succeed. Tell them what to study and how to study.

Praise again and tell them how smart they are.

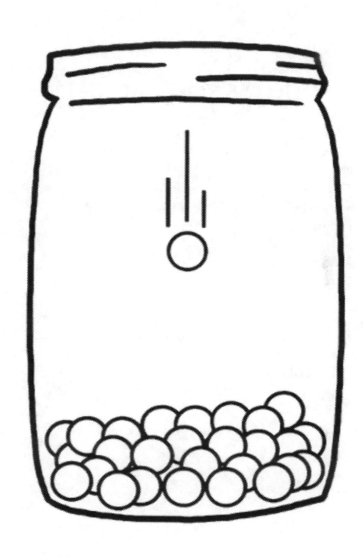

QUOTES YOU CAN USE.

"You are getting your tests back today. What a smart class. Your test papers were wonderful. Some people, however, have to study more."

"Remember one of our posted rules. No eating during class time." If I don't eat, you can't eat."

"Assignments are due in tomorrow. Check your spelling, grammar, and neatness."

"Friday, we are having a test on what we have covered in this unit. On the board are the items that you are expected to know for the test."

"For those questions that are missed, your homework will be to write the correct answer in a sentence or redo the problem correctly."

"A major part of your grade is what you have learned as shown by your test paper."

"See these jars with your period number on them? When everyone is quietly working, you will hear a 'clink' sound. That is a marble or poker chip being dropped in the jar. When there are 50 in the jar your class gets a treat reward. No chips or marbles will ever be taken out." Cookies are an appropriate treat. This is called assertive discipline and it works. Many teachers will say the kids should be good without a reward. Yes, but peer pressure works wonders. 50 "chips" in the jar should take several weeks. It works. I speak from experience.

PROBLEM SOLVING

Discuss the problem with the student.
Try rewards. Try consequences.
Meet with the assisant principal.
Conference with assistant principal, student, and sometimes a parent.
POSSIBLE PROBLEMS that you will encounter in your classroom:

TARDIES: follow the school policy on tardies. Detention after school does help. One solution is that the principal or assistant principal will assign detention for tardies to a particular room. This room is supervised by a teacher who selects the assignment in lieu of yard duty. Some teachers feel this beats being on the yard (campus). You must call the parents. Tardies is an ongoing issue among staff every year.

TALKING in class during instruction. Of course this is a problem, a daily problem. One method that works is the famous or is it the infamous checks on the board. One and two checks are warnings. You have acknowledged the student and problem. Three checks you call the parent and assign detention with you at lunch or after school. Of course you realize that you have put yourself in detention as well. With after school coaching, student council activities and yearbook which you may be involved in, detention can be a hardship on yourself. If nothing else works, a discipline referral to the office may be the only thing left to do. That is the fourth check.

As mentioned before in this book, it should be the last resort. It is not too long before "the office" says "not another one from THAT classroom. geez."

FIGHTING in the classroom can happen, although rarely. There may be an altercation on the yard between classes or at lunch and you are the "lucky" teacher to have them the next period. You must attempt to break up the fight and at the same time call the office. Sometime you can have a student call the office while you keep the combatants apart. They must be taken to the vice principal (sometimes called the assistant principal) at once and in the majority of cases will be suspended. A call to the parents by you is very important at their home or their work.

ASSIGNMENT not attempted by the student. He/she might have his/her head on the desk. Sometime you may have student who will just sit and do nothing. You must have a one on one talk to this person AND a call home to the parents. A talk with the school counselor about the student may shed some light on the problem. Also, see if other teachers have this same problem with the student.

INAPPROPRIATE CLOTHES worn by one of your students. Check school dress code policies and send the student to the "office". Office can be the vice principal, nurse, or counselor (if you have counselors at your school). If you do, become acquainted with the counselors. They can help you a great deal. The student's parent will be called to bring appropriate clothes. If not, there may be clean P.E. clothes to change into.

NO HOMEWORK. A call home is necessary. Often you will hear, "My child says you don't give homework." Explain your homework policy.

It rarely happens, but a student may "talk back" to you. Do not get in to an argument in front of the other students. This student should be sent to the "office" for the remainder of the period. You must call the parent. You must also talk to the student in private or with the assistant principal or counselor present. The student will surely go home and tell his parents a completely different story than what really happened.

Do not lose your temper and yell at the class. For poor homework, failing tests, not paying attention, and a variety of other reasons it is very tempting to shout at all of them. Better to reprimand the class in a stern but quiet manner. Do not swear. Talk to them about promotion, graduation, and losing school priveleges. Priveleges may include; attending dances, special assemblies, and special outdoor events. As mentioned previously, remind the class that they are not getting 50 "chips" in the jar for a treat. The kids will say for example, "Mrs. Roberts always yells."

Take away cell phones, hand held games, etc. Take away anything that distracts the student and class from the task at hand which is learning. You may return it to them after class, afterschool, after a week, or to a parent only. You decide how severe the problem is. Follow school rules and district policy.

PARENT CONFERENCES AND PHONE CALLS

Poor grades, bad conduct, no homework phone call.

"Hello, Mr./Mrs. _____. This is (Your Name) from (Name of your school) calling to let you know that I'm concerned about your child's progress in my (Name of Subject) class. With both of us working together I'm sure we can get your child to improve."

Not: "Your child is disruptive, he wrecks my class."

Then make your recommendations to the parent. Tell the student in your class what you told the parent.

PARENT CONFERENCES

Sign in sheet for parents. Name, phone number.

Be prepared. Be confident, not nervous!

Be able to explain the student's grades.

Have sample work from the student.

Show exemplary work to indicate the goal.

Say something nice about the student, first.

Explain how the student can improve or maintain the high grade.

Explain your expectations for the class that the child is in.

Remember there are people waiting, acknowledge them with a smile.

Most of the time the parent conferences will be in your classroom with just you and the parent(s).

At night, conferences can be held in the library or gym where all the teachers and parents convene.

You will have your name and class on a sign. Parents will wait their turn to talk to you. Be prepared! Bring gradebook and assignments!

In your classroom you sit and wait. You are prepared. You wonder who is going to show up. You are hoping that you see many parents. Who is going to be first.

You are thinking, "should I sit at my desk or sit at a table."

"Hi, how are you? I'm glad you made time to come see me."

You notice mom is upset about low grades in your class as well as poor citizenship grades. "Please sign in. Your name, phone number and your child's full name." You need to do this because many of your students' last names are different from their parent's name. You proceed to show the student's test grades, missed assignments etc. The mom begins to cry and says that in a recent divorce settlement her son/daughter stays at the ex husband's house every other week. "While I make sure the homework and studying is done when he is with me, it is not the case when he is staying at my ex's house. He doesn't care and drinks too much." Wow, you think, there is more information in some parent conferences than I care to know. Believe it. In most conferences, however, the parent is very concerned about his/her child and sticks to the subject of tests, homework, promotion, and grades.

You wonder who will be next. "Hi, my straight 'A' child just loves your class." You smile, that is nice to hear. "Terrific student," you reply. I love to see those parents, but I must also see the students who are below average or failing.

BACK TO SCHOOL NIGHT
OPEN HOUSE

Generally speaking, Back to School Night is in the Fall and Open House is in the Spring.

On Back to School Night your program, requirements, and expectations are laid out. Be clear on what you expect from your students.

BACK TO SCHOOL NIGHT

Back to School Night may follow a bell schedule so that you will see each class for less than 10 minutes.

Be well prepared for parents and dress accordingly.

You may ask their names or their child's name as they walk in or when class begins. It is a good idea to know who is there. You should make a note in your gradebook if the parent was present. It could be important later in the year for many reasons.

"Mrs. Morgan, had you been to school on Back To School Night, you would know the requirements and why your child is failing. You would also know the homework policy for my classes."

Show student work and show your textbook.

Tell parents how grades are achieved, your classwork assignments, and homework policy.

Make sure walls are decorated with your subject.

Display student work. Be enthused about your subject and class. You may want to invite the principal or assistant principal to one of your class presentations.

As a new teacher, having relatives present is not recommended as it could result in your being more nervous. Your presentation should be well prepared and organized. Do not run over your scheduled time as parents will be late to the next class. In your school, you may not have a schedule time so parents can visit as long as they wish.

As you will see on the next page, in the spring there is generally no set schedule. Parents will come and go. "Where does my child sit?"

"Is this his work?" You explain that work is from all your classes and may not be at the place where their child sits in that class.

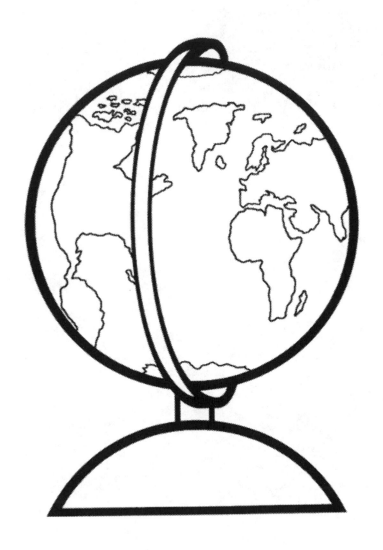

SPRING OPEN HOUSE

Many teachers will dread Open House and will readily talk against it. Remember reading this when you hear that talk in the Spring. Ignore that negative talk! Many teachers feel that Open House is a waste of time. "It's too late in the year" or "parents that need to come don't show up." However, that feeling is derived from low parent turnouts in their past experiences and a lack of enthusiasm for their subject. Why is it that (insert name of teacher) never shows up on Open House? He/she has been 'sick' on that day for the last ten years. Funny, it's the same sickness for Back to School and Parent Conferences. This does occur and of course it is unprofessional and hurts the image of the school and the teaching profession.

Open House is a great opportunity to show off what your students and of course what YOU have done.

It is a time to be proud and stand tall. Often a District Office administrator will visit, giving you a chance to show your expertise. It also gives you a chance to praise your students, classes, school, and administration.

You may put end of year promotion/graduation requirements on the board.

To those parents whose child has performed poorly, discuss what needs to be done for that student to be promoted or graduate.

If you hope to teach next year, it is a great opportunity to get parents to like your work. Maybe a parent will request another sibling for your class next year and call the office for that request.

YARD DUTY

Most everyone disdains yard duty especially on hot, cold, rainy, and busy in the classroom days. However, yard duty is a necessary obligation. Check your post map and dates. Circle them in red or highlight for your binder or wall.

Do not forget and be on time. You are the responsible person in case of an accident or a fight.

Students may run and get hurt. Make sure you are where you are supposed to be.

Do not bring the newspaper, papers to grade, or your lesson planner to yard duty. You are to watch the students. Circulate! If students see a teacher, they will stay out of trouble. Do not take a few minutes "off" to grab a snack or coffee. That is the time for sure, there will be a major problem where you were supposed to be. This can result in major trouble for you.

In case of a fight, tell someone to get an administrator as you attempt to stop the fight. Students can be very angry, so be careful. Also, do not grab a student in inappropriate places. You don't want to be sued. Ask your principal for actions by you that he/she would deem appropriate.

If you must miss yard duty, trade with a colleague. Tell your principal ahead of time. Common excuses for missing yard duty. "I have important work in the classroom".

"It's too cold". "I did not arrive to school on time."

"A parent wanted a conference".

"I'm not feeling well". "I was on the phone".

"I forgot". "I was talking to another teacher."

No excuses will be accepted. Prepare in advance.

FOR A HAPPY, PRODUCTIVE YEAR

Remember each day is a new beginning.

Don't dwell on the negative.

Don't "make a mountain out of a mole hill".

On educational issues, use YOUR best judgement.

Be honest and truthful.

Keep your expectations high, yet have empathy for those hard workers who have underachieved.

Do not accept poor quality work.

Follow all school procedures correctly.

Be friendly with the faculty. Make it a point to know everyone on the staff.

Do not continually complain or whine.

Volunteer for supervision of extra curricular activities.

Go to sporting events, dances, special events.

Be involved and love your school.

Do not cause the principal or assistant more grief.

Send home plenty of information about your class.

Be prepared for your observation by the principal.

Find out if your principal gives you a date for the observation or if it is unannounced.

Don't humiliate your students.

Use video, audio, and software to support learning.

Have rules for use of the computers.

Find ways to make your class a continued positive experience for you and your students.

Do not allow bathroom passes unless you feel it is extremely urgent. Jot down the time the student left your class. If you are lenient in letting students leave your classroom, you will discover that alot more students are asking for bathroom passes.

SO, YOU THINK YOU CAN TEACH MIDDLE SCHOOL

End Of Year Evaluation

Your principal will set up a time for you to come in to his office and discuss your evaluation. The evaluation is based on formal observations made in your classroom either announced or unannounced as previously discussed in this book.

There are many factors considered in your evaluation. Among the most common are I. Instruction 2. Classroom Management 3. Communication with parents, students, and staff. 4.Professional Responsibilities 5. Future Goals

You walk towards the principal's office after his secretary tells you he/she is waiting for you. "What will he/she tell me," you think. Did the principal like my teaching techniques? Did he/she like the lesson when he made a classroom visit? "Are my classes too noisy? Were all the students working? Can I manage my students? Do I contact parents? Have I complained in the staff room at lunch? Did I volunteer to coach a sport or two and did I supervise dances? Was there a club or activity I should have directed? Have I missed yard duty?

The main question, Will I be hired next year to this school that I've grown to love?

I have learned so much from the staff and the students. In many cases I have learned from the students as much as I have taught them.

After I have received the evaluation I ask that main question. Hopefully, the answer to you is, "We would love to have you back next year." Sometimes it's, "We have to wait for enrollment projections for next year and the budget. We'll let you know."You leave the principal's office with a heavy heart hoping that you will be rehired.

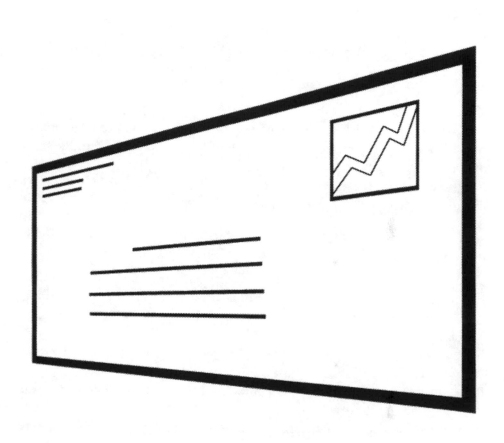

A LETTER TO YOUR STUDENTS

To my students,

You are about to enter a new part of your life that is very important and very exciting. It is a part of your life that will shape your future and the kind of person that you will grow up to be.

I have put together some advice that will make life easier for you and make you a success in school and life.

IN THE CLASSROOM:

Follow classroom rules. Each teacher has different rules and expectations.

Pay attention to the teacher at all times. Listen carefully. If there is something that you do not understand, raise your hand or talk to the teacher after class.

Never cheat on a test or classwork, or give anyone else your answers helping them cheat.

Respect all your classmates of different races, abilities, and backgrounds. You respect them, they will respect you.

Be prepared for each class, every day! Have your books, papers, and assignments ready. Do not make excuses.

Do not talk to other students during the times the teacher wants your attention or wants the class quiet.

Be organized. Have an organized binder and notebook.

IN THE SCHOOLYARD

Be on time to class when the bell rings. Never be tardy!

Do not talk about other students or spread stories.

Never lose your temper in a game. Play hard & fair.

Do not bully others and do not allow anyone to bully you. Report it to the principal or teacher.

Stay in bounds and never go off campus or where students are not allowed.

Follow all school rules.

Do not bring anything to school that is against the rules.

Tell a teacher or principal immediately if you see or hear of anything that could be dangerous to the school.

Never go home with anyone unless you tell your parents first.

Be a friend to all students.

AT HOME

Make sure you have a quiet, well lighted place for your homework. Set aside time each day for homework and study. Make sure you complete the assignment every day without having to be reminded by your parents. Have it neat and ready to be handed in. Make sure you plan your day to allow homework time.

Have your clothes ready the night before school.

Review a lesson from class.

Please keep these two pages in your notebook or in your room where you can see them everyday.

SO, NOW YOU THINK YOU CAN TEACH MIDDLE SCHOOL?

The answer, of course, is yes. You have taken this book seriously and followed the advice. You are going to be a second year teacher and you are excited that you finished your first year. Unlike in some sports, there is no second year "slump". Of course you will learn more in your second year. The mistakes that you made will not be made again.

You have experienced the highs and lows of the classroom. You have had wonderful days and days that you cried when you went home. "What went wrong today?" you think outloud. "I can't let that happen again." You have experienced the frustration of your students not understanding the lesson that you worked so hard to prepare. "Why were the test grades so poor when my lessons were so good?" You have experienced exhilaration on days when your students were so good and the classwork and tests were excellent. What a great feeling of accomplishment. You were professional at meetings and did not listen to the complainers who always say this meeting is a waste of time.

You were a positive influence rather than being negative. Somehow, in middle school the negativity is more prevalent than at any other level. It only serves to drag down the entire morale of the school. You established good rapport with the principal and other school and district administrators. They got to know you as an excellent teacher. No parent challenged your grading system or your assessment of their child's progress. Among the teachers you established a camaraderie. You didn't listen to the ones who said, "Why did you become a teacher?"

Thank goodness the vast majority of teachers are positive and extremely dedicated. Many face hardships of small budgets and deteriorating classrooms, poor lighting, etc. But thankfully this is no longer the norm in most places.

You show by example that your friends are misguided when they say you could have been a doctor, or a lawyer or whatever. "There is not enough pay" they continue to say. "You can't live on that salary." "You couldn't pay me enough to teach middle school." But then, who would teach their children?!

In conclusion, yes you can teach middle school. You loved those kids. You have made a difference in their lives. They will remember you for it and thank you. Remember, TO TEACH IS TO TOUCH A LIFE FOREVER. You did.

APPENDIX

I

Your notes before you report to school.

what I need to buy for my desk.

visit the teachers' supply store or an office supply store.

what bulletin board material can I use.

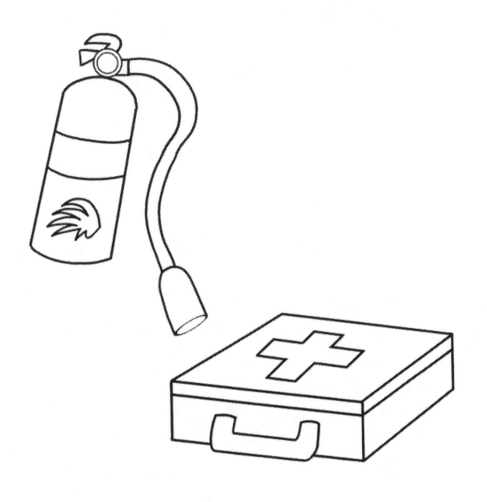

II

Orientation faculty meeting notes.

yard duty schedule and your post

discipline policies

emergency procedures

testing schedule

more

III

Department meeting notes:

supplies

units to be covered

textbooks

software

computer use and internet rules

department meeting dates

dates of future meetings

IV

CLASSROOM BUDGET

estimate your budget needs for your classes and when to purchase these items.

allow six to eight weeks if ordering from vendors.

plan ahead

software, dvd's, etc.

keep receipts

V

Staff you may need to contact.

e mail

phone

address

Sometimes questions occur when you are home. You do not want to call the administrators.

VI

Lessons that worked.

objectives met

class excited

assignments done

VII

Lessons that did not work.

poor homework

class obviously bored

poor test grades

students complained

unit took too long

VIII

Extra curricular activities.

I signed up to direct the following student activities.

I will supervise the following activities.

activity and date.

IX

Substitute information.

Follow school policy on retaining a substitute for your class. Time of your call and day is important.

Name of substitutes that I would prefer in my classroom

X

Substitute information that should be on your desk.

Arrive at school and in your classroom 30-40 minutes before the first bell.

Door must be locked upon leaving the room.

Yard duty schedule and your post should be clear.

All necessary materials to help make for a successful day must be clearly visible.

The "sub" should write his/her name clearly on the chalkboard if there is one.

Have class list and seating chart on your desk. Since you never really know when you might become ill at home, the class list and seating arrangement MUST be on your desk when you leave school each day. A good idea is to have a binder containing both.

At the end of the day, all doors and windows are to be locked before the substitute leaves the classroom and turns the room key into the office.

Leave the name of a teacher close by for help.

Be well planned and assignments can be collected at the end of class.

Have the teacher leave a detailed message of what was and was not covered on that day.

Lack of adhering to the advice on this page can lead to your class being in disarray when you return.

XI

Evaluation at the end of the year.

The following components establish criteria for your evaluation. This is an example. School districts may differ on their evaluation form.

Instruction: has high expectations, has diagnosed student needs clearly, uses effective teaching strategies, to name a few.

Classroom management: communicates clearly, maintains accurate records, implements a good discipline program, organizes classroom for effective learning.

Parent communications: notes, telephone calls, email, and report cards keep parents informed.

Staff: promotes a collegial spirit as a team member of the staff.

Professional responsibilities: assists with student activities, demonstrates professional growth, and displays a positive, responsible attitude.

Congratulations on your terrific evaluation. I am glad you selected this book that helped you get through the year.

You're successful. Bring on next year!